THE SEVEN WONDERS
OF THE ANCIENT WORLD

Reg Cox & Neil Morris

Belitha Press

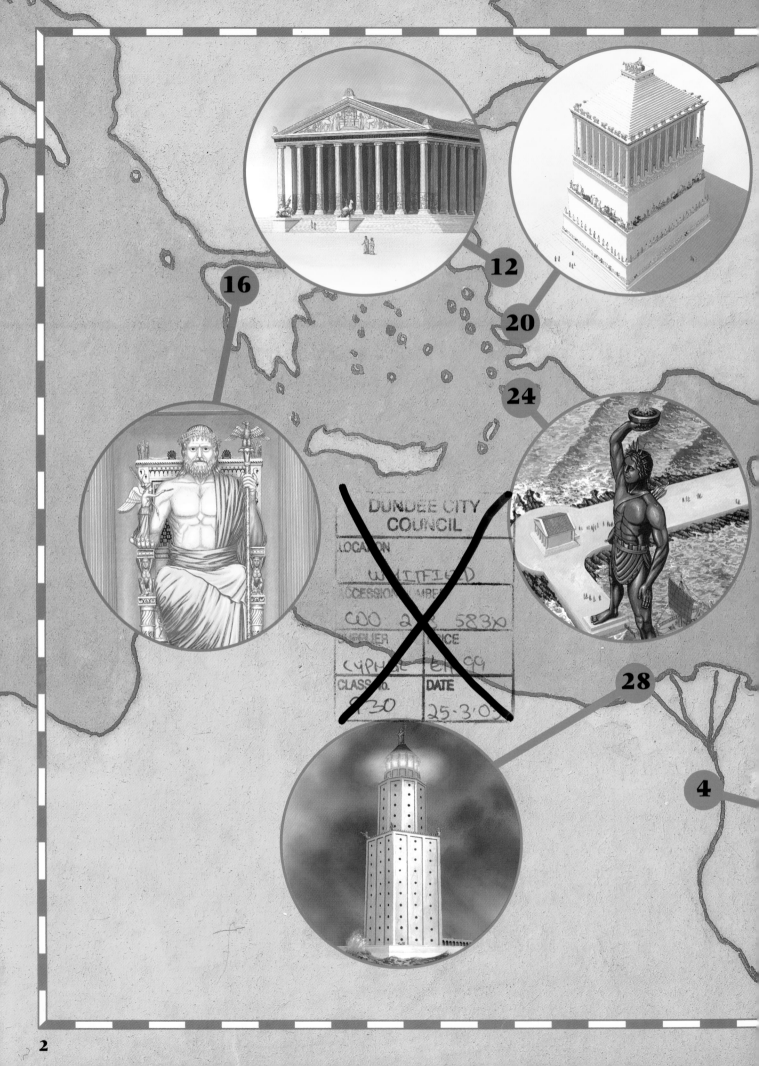

INTRODUCTION

Over 2,000 years ago, writers began to list the amazing buildings and structures they had seen or heard of. In about 120 BC, a Greek poet called Antipater of Sidon wrote about seven such places. They could all be found in a small region around the eastern Mediterranean – an area the ancient Greek writers knew well. Few had travelled beyond it. Perhaps the list was a kind of tourist guide. The list of wonders has survived to this day, even though only one of the structures still stands. They are known as the Seven Wonders of the Ancient World.

CONTENTS

8

Words in bold are explained in the glossary on page 32.

THE GREAT PYRAMID AT GIZA

This vast Egyptian pyramid is the oldest of the Seven Wonders of the Ancient World. It is also the only wonder still standing today. When it was built, the Great Pyramid was the tallest structure in the world. And it probably held that record for almost 4,000 years.

A ROYAL TOMB

The Great Pyramid was built as a tomb for Khufu, known to the Greeks as Cheops. He was one of the **pharaohs**, or kings of ancient Egypt, and his tomb was finished in about 2580 BC.

Later, two more pyramids were built at Giza, for Khufu's son and grandson, as well as smaller pyramids for their queens. Khufu's pyramid is the furthest away in this picture and is the biggest. His son's pyramid is in the middle and looks taller because it stands on higher ground.

BUILDING THE PYRAMID

The pyramids stand in an ancient **cemetery** at Giza, on the opposite bank of the River Nile from Cairo, the capital of modern Egypt. Some **archaeologists** think that it may have taken 100,000 men over 20 years to build the Great Pyramid. It was made from more than 2 million stone blocks, each weighing 2.5 tonnes or more. The workers hauled these into place using ramps, rollers and levers, and then fitted them together without using **mortar**.

GLEAMING LIMESTONE

When the main structure was complete, it looked like a series of steps. These were then filled in with blocks of white limestone, which were cut to give a smooth, gleaming surface. They fitted so closely that a knife blade could not be pushed between the blocks on the outside. When this was finished, the Great Pyramid rose to a height of 147 metres. Its top is now missing, and today only Khufu's son's pyramid has any limestone covering left at the top. The Great Pyramid measures 230 metres along each side of its base. It covers an area bigger than nine football pitches.

BURYING THE PHARAOH

The ancient Egyptians believed that when a person died, the body had to be looked after, so that the spirit could live on after death. They took out the internal organs, packed the body with salts and wrapped it in linen bandages. This preserved the body as a **mummy**. The mummy was then buried with clothes, food, jewellery and other things that would be useful in the afterlife. Khufu's mummified body was placed in a **burial chamber** deep inside his pyramid.

In contrast to his huge pyramid, the only known figure of Khufu is a tiny ivory statue.

A statue of Khufu's grandson, Menkaure, builder of the third pyramid. He is flanked by goddesses.

The pyramids today. Their white limestone covering was stripped off centuries ago, to be used for buildings in Cairo.

Khafre, son of Khufu. In this statue, he is guarded by the god Horus, who has taken the shape of a falcon.

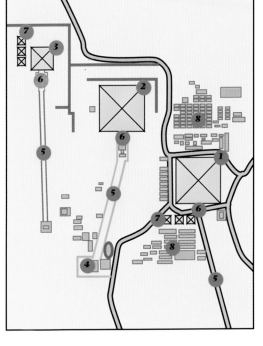

A plan of the pyramids of Khufu (1), Khafre (2) and Menkaure (3). Each pyramid had a valley temple (4), where the pharaoh's body was probably mummified. A long causeway (5) led to a mortuary temple (6), where offerings were made to the pharaoh's spirit. Nearby were the queens' pyramids (7) and the rectangular tombs (8) of Khufu's relatives and courtiers.

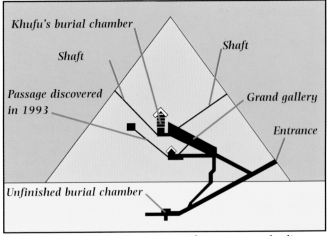

Khufu's burial chamber

Shaft

Shaft

Passage discovered in 1993

Grand gallery

Entrance

Unfinished burial chamber

Inside and beneath the Great Pyramid are passages leading to chambers, including the pharaoh's burial chamber.

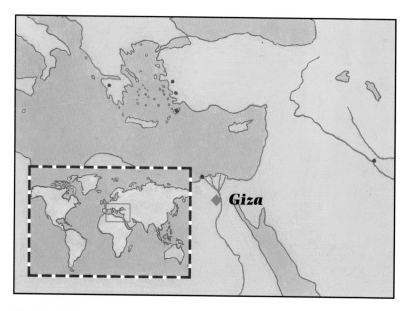

Giza

Khufu's black granite **sarcophagus**, or stone coffin. It probably held a wooden coffin with the pharaoh's body inside.

This wooden boat was found buried in a pit near the Great Pyramid. It has been put together and can be seen at the site today. The boat may have been used to carry Khufu's body across the Nile. Or it may have been a 'sun boat' to ferry his spirit across the heavens.

The pyramids were built in layers of stone blocks. Each layer was a bit smaller than the one before. The stones were probably dragged up a huge earth ramp, which was made higher for each layer.

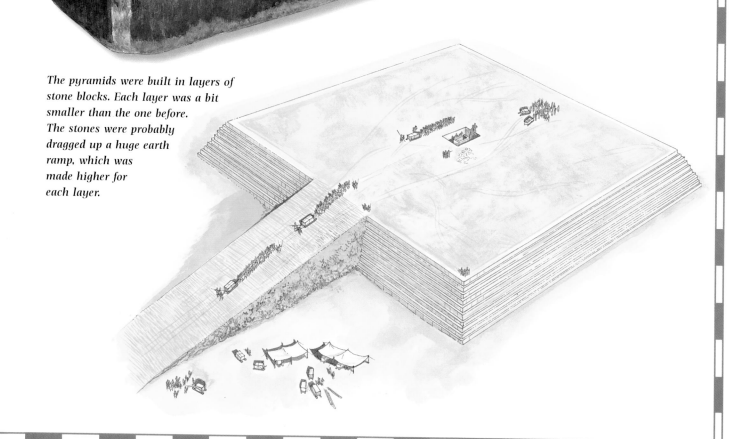

THE HANGING GARDENS OF BABYLON

The Hanging Gardens were one of the most famous features of the ancient city of Babylon. But although archaeologists have found ruins that may be from the gardens, they cannot be sure. We only know that they existed because people saw them and wrote about them.

NEBUCHADNEZZAR AND AMYTIS

Greek and Roman writers tell us that the gardens were built in about 600 BC on the orders of Nebuchadnezzar II, King of Babylon. This great city lay on the banks of the River Euphrates, south of present-day Baghdad, the capital of modern Iraq. One story says that the king had the gardens built for his homesick young wife, Amytis, to remind her of her home in the mountains of Persia.

WATERED TERRACES

The Hanging Gardens were probably built near the river, overlooking Babylon's city walls. They were made up of **terraces**, and the top terrace may have been up to 40 metres above the ground. Nebuchadnezzar had the gardens planted with every kind of tree and plant that can be imagined. These were brought from all over the empire by ox-cart and river-barge. Figs, almonds, walnut trees, pomegranates, rock roses, waterlilies and incense bushes may all have grown in the garden.

The success of the gardens must have depended on a good watering system, using water drawn from the Euphrates. The water may have been lifted to the top terrace by a chain of buckets driven by slaves on a **treadmill**. It could then run down into the streams and waterfalls in the gardens and keep the soil wet.

A stone carving of Ishtar, the Babylonians' most important goddess. She was the goddess of love and war, and her lions decorated the city of Babylon.

The city was entered through the huge Ishtar Gate, named after the goddess. The gate was covered with glazed blue bricks, and decorated with yellow and brown bulls and dragons.

Babylon was **excavated** in the early twentieth century. The site had been reduced to such a low level that the buildings were hard to reconstruct.

This plan of Babylon shows where we think the Hanging Gardens may have been (1). The Processional Way (2) led through the Ishtar Gate (3) into the walled city to Nebuchadnezzar's palace (4). Shortly after Nebuchadnezzar's reign, the city was taken over by the Persians.

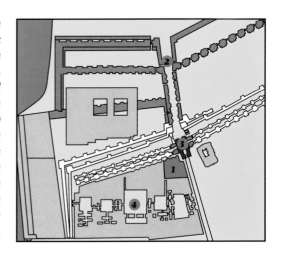

This tablet lists plants in an earlier royal garden. Plants were a source of food and medicine.

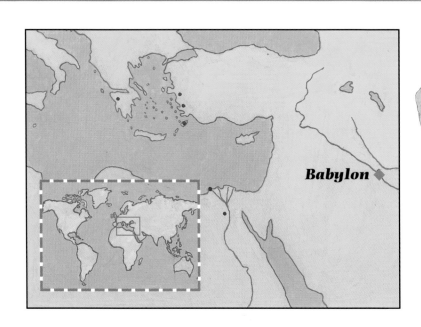

This lion-headed monster probably represents Marduk, the Babylonians' main god. Every year they held a festival to Marduk.

A clay tablet showing an ancient map of the world, as it was known at that time. Babylon was first settled around 3000 BC. From about 2000 BC, the Babylonians established a large and powerful empire.

Lions on the Processional Way leading to the Ishtar Gate. At the New Year festival, people walked along the Way from the Temple of Marduk, carrying a statue of the god.

THE TEMPLE OF ARTEMIS AT EPHESUS

This coin was produced in Ephesus in the third century AD. It shows how the temple looked.

C roesus was the last king of Lydia, a region of ancient Asia Minor that is part of present-day Turkey. He was famous for his great wealth, and in 560 BC he had a magnificent temple built at Ephesus. This city had been founded thousands of years before. According to legend, the founders were Amazons, a race of women warriors.

THE BIGGEST MARBLE TEMPLE

Croesus decided to build the temple in honour of the goddess of the moon and protector of animals and young girls. The Greeks called her Artemis, the Romans called her Diana. The temple was made of limestone and marble, which workmen quarried in the nearby hills.

The main structure of the temple was supported by about 120 marble columns. Each vast column was 20 metres high. The huge blocks that made up the columns had to be hauled into place by **pulleys** and were held together by metal pegs. Once the roof had been put on, artists completed the building with beautiful sculptures and decorations. A statue of Artemis stood in the middle of the temple.

This was one of the largest temples of the **classical world**, much bigger than the **Parthenon**, which was built later at Athens. The platform on which it was built was 131 metres long and 79 metres wide.

HEROSTRATUS AND ALEXANDER

Two hundred years later, in 356 BC, the temple was burned to the ground. The fire was started by a man called Herostratus, who simply wanted to make himself famous. Strangely, the temple was destroyed on the very day that Alexander the Great was born. Some years later, Alexander visited Ephesus and gave orders for the temple to be rebuilt on the same site.

FINAL DESTRUCTION

Alexander's temple survived until the third century AD. Gradually the harbour at Ephesus silted up and the town became less important. The temple was **plundered** by **Goths** and later swamped by floods. All that is left of the temple at Ephesus today are a few foundation blocks and a single rebuilt column.

This life-size marble statue of Artemis was found in the ancient city hall at Ephesus. To the Ephesians she was a mother goddess.

A sculpture from one of the temple's columns. The beauty of the temple attracted pilgrims from all over the Mediterranean world.

A small ivory statue of a priestess of Artemis from the seventh century BC. Many visitors to the temple bought souvenirs made by local craftsmen, such as small statues of the goddess Artemis.

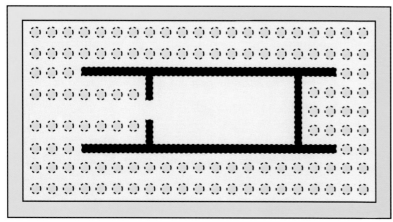

This plan of the temple shows the supporting columns and the large room where a statue of the goddess Artemis stood.

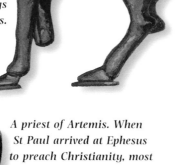

A stag found at the site. The stag was sacred to Artemis. Her chariot was drawn by white stags with golden horns.

Only a single column of the temple stands today. This was rebuilt from the ruins in recent years. But there are many other remains of the once great city — a ruined theatre, a library, baths and many other public buildings.

A priest of Artemis. When St Paul arrived at Ephesus to preach Christianity, most priests and craftsmen tried to shout him down because he threatened their livelihood.

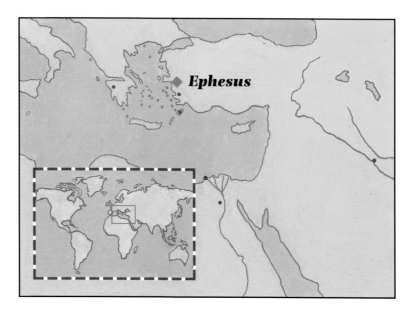

Ephesus

THE STATUE OF ZEUS AT OLYMPIA

Almost 3,000 years ago, Olympia was an important religious centre in south-west Greece. The ancient Greeks worshipped Zeus, king of the gods, and held regular festivals there in his honour. These included athletic competitions. The first Olympic Games, as they came to be known, were probably held in 776 BC. For over 1100 years, the games then took place every four years. They were very important and all wars had to stop to allow competitors and spectators to attend the games.

THE TEMPLE OF ZEUS
In the fifth century BC, the citizens of Olympia decided to build a temple to Zeus. A magnificent structure was put up between the years 466 and 456 BC. It was built with huge stone blocks surrounded by massive columns. For some years after it was finished, the temple had no proper statue of Zeus, and it was soon decided that this was needed. A famous sculptor from Athens was chosen to make the statue.

BUILDING THE STATUE
The sculptor's name was Pheidias, and in Athens he had already made two magnificent statues of the goddess **Athena**. At Olympia, Pheidias and his workmen first put up a wooden framework, to act as a skeleton for Zeus. They then covered this with plates of ivory for the god's skin and sheets of gold for his clothing. The workers covered up the joins so that the finished statue looked like a solid figure.

HIGH ABOVE THE GROUND
Zeus was seated on a throne **inlaid** with ebony and precious stones. The finished statue was 13 metres high and reached almost to the ceiling of the temple. It gave the impression that if Zeus stood up, he would lift off the roof. Viewing platforms were built along the walls so that people could climb up and see the god's face. When it was completed around 435 BC, the statue stood as one of the world's greatest wonders for the next 800 years.

MOVING THE STATUE
In about AD 40, the Roman emperor Caligula wanted to have the statue moved to Rome. Workers were sent to collect it, but according to legend the statue let out such a bellow of laughter that the workers fled. Then in AD 391, with the rise of Christianity, the Romans banned the Olympic Games and closed the Greek temples. Some years later, the statue of Zeus was shipped to Constantinople. In AD 462 the palace containing the statue was destroyed by fire, leaving nothing behind.

The whole area of Olympia was shaken by earthquakes in the sixth century. The temple and stadium were destroyed by landslides and floods, and the remains were covered by mud. This helped to preserve certain parts of Olympia for over a thousand years. In recent times archaeologists have uncovered the site. Now people can walk around the ruins of the temple and see where the magnificent statue of Zeus once stood. The statue itself is gone for ever.

The Roman ring above, made of a gemstone called carnelian, is engraved with the statue of Zeus in its temple.

The remains of the temple of Zeus, as we can see them today. The site was excavated in recent times.

Olympia was in the ancient Greek state of Elis. This coin from Elis shows the statue of Zeus on its reverse side.

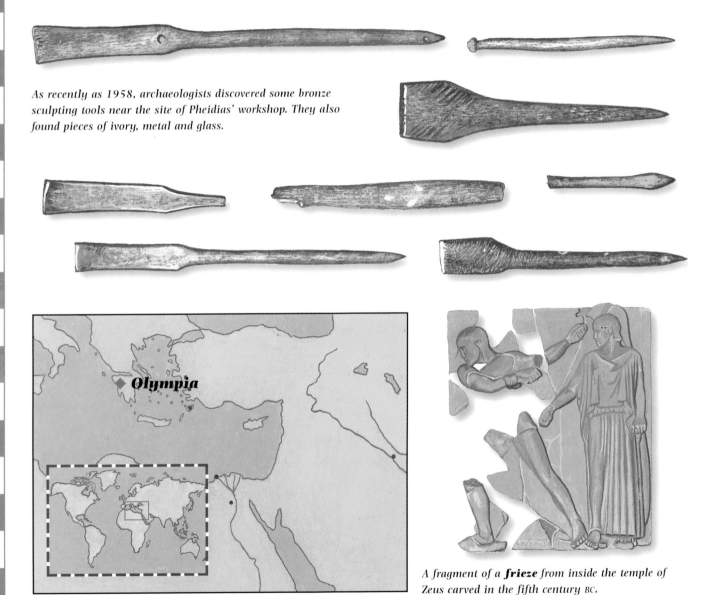

As recently as 1958, archaeologists discovered some bronze sculpting tools near the site of Pheidias' workshop. They also found pieces of ivory, metal and glass.

Olympia

A fragment of a *frieze* from inside the temple of Zeus carved in the fifth century BC.

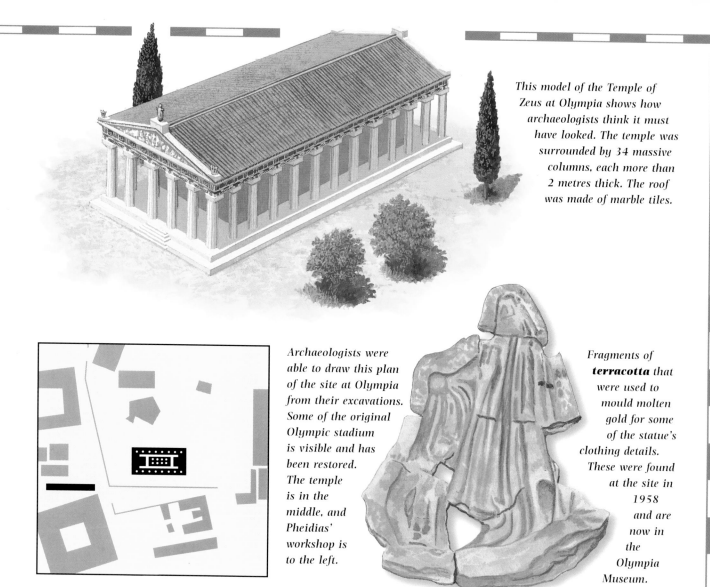

This model of the Temple of Zeus at Olympia shows how archaeologists think it must have looked. The temple was surrounded by 34 massive columns, each more than 2 metres thick. The roof was made of marble tiles.

Archaeologists were able to draw this plan of the site at Olympia from their excavations. Some of the original Olympic stadium is visible and has been restored. The temple is in the middle, and Pheidias' workshop is to the left.

Fragments of **terracotta** that were used to mould molten gold for some of the statue's clothing details. These were found at the site in 1958 and are now in the Olympia Museum.

A plaque from a sculptured frieze that ran around the walls of the temple. The frieze shows the 12 labours of Herakles. Athena looks on, as Atlas offers golden apples. Herakles, in the middle, is holding up the world on his shoulders. Herakles and Athena were both children of Zeus.

THE MAUSOLEUM AT HALICARNASSUS

ausolus was ruler of Caria, part of the Persian Empire, from 377 to 353 BC. The region's capital was Halicarnassus, which is now a tourist centre in modern Turkey, called Bodrum. Mausolus had followed his father as ruler, and as provincial governor to the King of Persia. But he broke free of the Persians and acted as an independent king.

THE ORIGINAL MAUSOLEUM

Mausolus married his sister, Artemisia. As he grew more powerful, he planned a tomb for himself and his queen. But this was to be no ordinary tomb. Mausolus wanted a magnificent monument that would remind the world of his wealth and power long after he had died.

Mausolus died before his tomb was finished, but his widow supervised the building until it was complete, in about 350 BC. It was called the **Mausoleum**, after the king, and this word is still used for any large stately tomb.

LIONS GUARD THE CHAMBER

The royal couple's ashes were put in golden caskets in a burial chamber at the base of the building. A row of stone lions guarded the chamber. Above the solid stone base was a structure that looked like a Greek temple, surrounded by columns and statues. At the top of the building was a stepped pyramid. This was crowned, 43 metres above the ground, by the statue of a horse-drawn chariot. Statues of the king and queen probably rode in it.

DESTROYED BY EARTHQUAKE

Eighteen hundred years later, an earthquake shook the Mausoleum to the ground. In 1489 the Christian **Knights of St John** began using its stones to build a castle nearby. They built some of their castle walls from blocks of green stone that had formed the main part of the Mausoleum. Some years later the knights discovered the burial chamber of Mausolus and Artemisia. But when they left the chamber unguarded overnight, it was raided by pirates for its gold and other precious contents.

STATUES EXCAVATED

Another 300 years passed before archaeologists began to excavate the site. They dug up parts of the base of the Mausoleum, as well as the statues and sculptures that had not been broken up or stolen. Among these were the huge statues that archaeologists believe show the king and queen. In 1857 these were taken to the British Museum in London, where they can still be seen. There have been further excavations in recent years, and today there are just a few stones left at the site in Bodrum.

The statue of the lion above is among the treasures from the Mausoleum in the British Museum.

A chariot horse that stood at the top of the building. Its bridle is made of bronze.

Archaeologists believe that this huge statue found at the site is of King Mausolus himself.

A marble head from a statue of Apollo, Greek god of music, archery and healing, and twin brother of Artemis. This statue stood at the tomb.

This colossal statue from the Mausoleum is believed to be of Queen Artemisia.

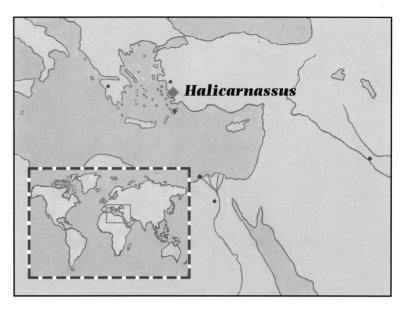

Halicarnassus

Stone blocks and parts of columns are all that remain at the site of the Mausoleum in modern-day Turkey.

Slabs of a Mausoleum frieze show Greeks battling against the Amazons, a race of women warriors. The figures, probably by the sculptor Scopas, are famous for the way they express emotion and movement.

THE COLOSSUS OF RHODES

he **Colossus** was a giant statue that stood at the city-port of Rhodes, in the Aegean Sea off present-day Turkey. In ancient times, the people of Rhodes wanted to be independent traders. They tried to stay out of other people's wars, but they were conquered many times.

HELIOS, THE SUN GOD

At the end of the fourth century BC, the people of Rhodes wanted to celebrate a victory. They had just successfully defended their city, on the island of Rhodes, against a year-long **siege** by Greek soldiers. The Greeks, realizing they could not win, had even left some of their battle equipment behind. The people of Rhodes decided to sell this equipment and build a statue of Helios, their sun god, to thank him for protecting them.

A BRONZE COLOSSUS

We do not know exactly what the statue looked like, or even where it stood. But we do know that it was made of bronze and was about 33 metres high. It was designed by an **architect** named Chares and took 12 years to build.

The face of Helios, the sun god, on a coin from Rhodes, dating from 200 BC.

ACROSS THE HARBOUR

The outer bronze shell was attached to an iron framework. The hollow statue was built from the ground up, and as it grew it was filled with stones to help it stand firmly. The Colossus was finished around 280 BC. For many centuries people believed that the Colossus towered across the entrance to Rhodes harbour, as shown opposite. This would have been impossible. The harbour mouth was about 400 metres across, and the statue was not quite so colossal. Writings suggest that it may have stood in the heart of the city, overlooking the sea and the harbour.

A COLOSSAL CRASH

In about 226 BC, little more than 50 years after it was completed, the Colossus fell. It was toppled by an earthquake and snapped off at the knees. The people of Rhodes were told by an **oracle** not to rebuild the statue, and so they left it lying where it fell. It stayed like this for nearly 900 years, and people would travel to Rhodes just to gaze at the ruins of the fallen sun god.

In AD 654 a Syrian prince captured Rhodes and stripped the statue of its bronze plates. People said that he took them back to Syria on the backs of 900 camels. The bronze was sold by merchants and probably turned into coins.

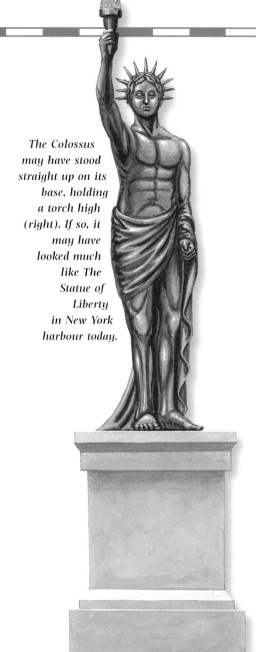

The Colossus may have stood straight up on its base, holding a torch high (right). If so, it may have looked much like The Statue of Liberty in New York harbour today.

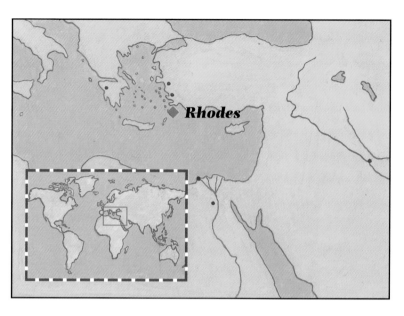

Rhodes

Demetrius, known as 'the Besieger', the Greek general who commanded the forces during the siege of Rhodes.

Demetrius attacked Rhodes with 200 warships and 40,000 soldiers. The most famous type of Greek warship was the trireme, with three banks of rowers on each side. This modern reconstruction was built to show how the oars were arranged. Soldiers fought on the flat deck of the boat.

The head of Helios. On the Colossus, metal sun rays may have been fitted into sockets in the god's hair.

Today, bronze deer stand on pillars at each side of the entrance to Rhodes harbour. Deer are an emblem of Rhodes, part of modern Greece.

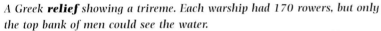

A Greek **relief** showing a trireme. Each warship had 170 rowers, but only the top bank of men could see the water.

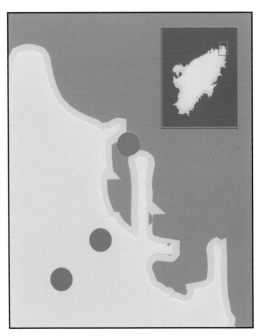

This map of the city of Rhodes shows three possible locations of the Colossus – across the harbour, near to it or in the city centre.

THE PHAROS OF ALEXANDRIA

I In the third century BC, a lighthouse was built to guide ships safely past the reefs into the harbour of Alexandria. It did this by reflecting the flames of a fire at night, and with a column of smoke by day. This was the world's first lighthouse, and it stood for 1,500 years.

ISLAND AND LIGHTHOUSE

The lighthouse was built on the small island of Pharos, in the Mediterranean Sea, off the city of Alexandria. This busy port was founded by Alexander the Great during his visit to Egypt. The building was named after the island. It must have taken about 20 years to build, and was completed in about 280 BC, during the reign of the Egyptian king, Ptolemy II.

Alexander the Great (356–323 BC), founder of Alexandria.

THREE TOWERS

The Pharos lighthouse was made up of three marble towers, built on a base of massive stone blocks. The first tower was rectangular and filled with rooms, where workers and soldiers lived. On top of that was a smaller, eight-sided tower, with a spiral ramp leading up to the top tower.

A GUIDING LIGHT

The top tower was shaped like a cylinder and in it burned the fire that guided boats safely into harbour. Standing on the top tower was a statue of Zeus the Saviour. The overall height of the Pharos was about 117 metres.

POLISHED BRONZE MIRROR

Huge amounts of fuel were needed to keep the fire alight. Wood was carried up the spiral ramp on carts pulled by horses or mules. Sheets of bronze stood behind the fire and reflected its light out to sea. Ships up to 50 kilometres away could see this beacon. By the twelfth century AD, the harbour at Alexandria had become so clogged with mud that it could no longer be used by ships. The lighthouse fell into disrepair. The sheets of bronze that had acted as mirrors were probably melted down for coins.

In the fourteenth century the Pharos was destroyed by an earthquake. Some years later Muslims used the ruins to build a military fort. This has been rebuilt since that time and still stands on the site of the world's first lighthouse.

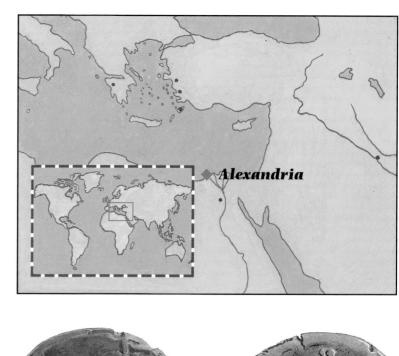

Alexandria

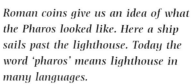

Roman coins give us an idea of what the Pharos looked like. Here a ship sails past the lighthouse. Today the word 'pharos' means lighthouse in many languages.

This coin, from the second century AD, clearly shows windows in the large lower section of the lighthouse.

This drawing suggests how the Pharos may have looked inside. It shows the fire in the top section and the ramp winding its way upwards.

The patron goddess of sailors, Isis, holds a ship's sail out towards the Pharos. She was one of Egypt's most popular goddesses.

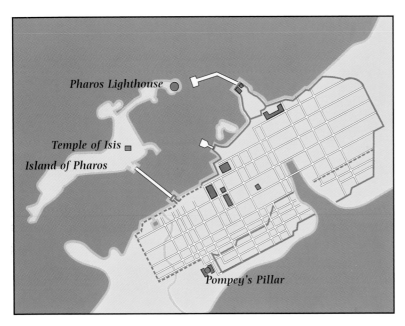

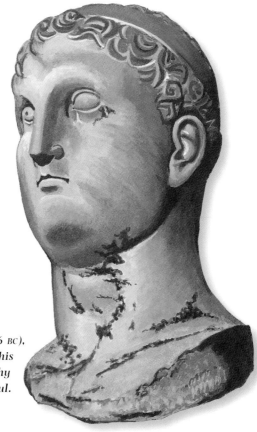

A map of ancient Alexandria as it was between the years 100 BC and AD 100. The former island of Pharos was then linked to the mainland by a causeway.

Ptolemy II (309–246 BC), King of Egypt. Under his rule, Egypt was wealthy and powerful.

An ancient incense burner in the shape of the Pharos. Incense was burnt for its fragrant scent, often in religious ceremonies.

Alexandria was a very important city in Roman times. This pillar, called Pompey's Pillar, and a sphinx are nearly all that remain from that period.

GLOSSARY

archaeologist: a person who studies the ancient past by digging up and looking at remains.

architect: a person who designs buildings.

Athena: the Greek goddess of war and wisdom.

burial chamber: a room where bodies were buried and kept.

cemetery: a burial ground.

classical world: the ancient Greek and Roman civilizations.

colossus: a huge object, especially a statue.

excavate: to dig up buried objects to find out about the past.

frieze: a story told in sculpture or pictures on the inside or outside of a building.

Goths: Germanic peoples from Scandinavia who invaded the Roman Empire from the third to the fifth century AD.

inlaid: set into prepared slots in a surface.

Knights of St John: a religious order of fighting monks.

mausoleum: originally the tomb of Mausolus, the word is now used for any large, stately tomb.

mortar: a cement-like mixture.

mummy: a body specially prepared and preserved before burial in Ancient Egypt.

oracle: a sacred place where a god foretold events, usually through a priest or priestess, and the prophesy itself.

Parthenon: a temple on the hill of the Acropolis in Athens, built betweeen 447 and 432 BC and dedicated to Athena.

pharaoh: the name given to kings of Ancient Egypt.

plunder: to steal valuable and sacred items by force.

pulley: a wheel with a grooved rim in which a rope can run. A set of pulleys can be used to lift heavy loads.

relief: figures and images cut into one side of a block of stone, so that they stand out from it.

sarcophagus: a tomb or coffin made of stone or marble.

siege: a military operation to capture a fortified place, by surrounding it, attacking it, and cutting off its supplies.

terrace: a flat area of ground cut into a slope.

terracotta: a reddish-brown baked clay.

treadmill: a wheel or cylinder, with footholds, that turned when men walked or trod on it.

INDEX

This edition published in 2002 by Belitha Press
A member of Chrysalis Books plc
64 Brewery Road, London N7 9NT

Copyright © in this format Belitha Press
Series devised by Reg Cox
Design copyright © Reg Cox
Text copyright © Neil Morris
Illustrations copyright © James Field

ISBN 1 84138 662 6

CIP Data for this book is available from the British Library

Printed in Hong Kong

Editor: Claire Edwards
Picture researcher: Juliet Duff
Consultant: Dr. Anne Millard

Picture acknowledgements: Ancient Art & Architecture: cover, 14 left, 15 top right, 23 centre right, 26 bottom, 31 bottom right. Bridgeman Art Library: 22 top left. Reg Cox: 27 top right. CM Dixon: 11 bottom right. Werner Forman Archive: 6 top right Dr Strouhal; 7 top right. Robert Harding Picture Library: 18 top left. Christine Osborne/Middle East Pix: 10 top right.